Irish Castles *and*
Fortified Houses

David Sweetman

Country House, Dublin

Published in 1995 by
Town House and Country House
Trinity House
Charleston Road
Ranelagh, Dublin 6
Ireland

British Library Cataloguing in Publication Data. A catalogue record for this book is available from the British Library.

ISBN: 0-946172-49-8

Illustration acknowledgements
The Office of Public Works, plates 1, 3, 5, 7, 10, 11, 12, 13, 14, 15, 16, 17, 18, and photos 4, 5, 6, 7, 9, 11, 12, 13, 14, 15, 16, 17; Kevin O'Brien, photo 1; David Johnson, plates 2, 4; David Sweetman, plate 6; John Scarry, plate 8; Katie Sweetman, photo 8; Conleth Manning, plate 9.

Cover: *Donegal Castle, Co Donegal*

Series editor: Michael Ryan
Text editor: Elaine Campion
Design & artwork: Bill and Tina Murphy
Colour origination: The Kulor Centre
Printed in Ireland by ßetaprint

CONTENTS

The piecemeal conquest of Ireland by the Anglo-Normans, which commenced in the year 1169, had a fundamental impact on the Irish landscape. By the time Prince John arrived in Ireland in 1185 the Anglo-Normans held the cities of Dublin, Waterford and Cork, along with their immediate hinterlands. Their military successes must be attributed to their fighting skill, especially on horseback, their organisation, and their ability to build strongholds (ie earthwork castles) rapidly in strategic positions. According to Gerald of Wales, whose *Conquest of Ireland* is a contemporary source for the early settlement, the Irish used bogs and woods for protection, and he also mentions round, ditched sites (ringforts) and walled sites (cashels).

The introduction by the Anglo-Normans of large earthwork and stone castles was something totally new to the Irish landscape. The castles can be divided roughly into three major groups: the earthwork castles of the earliest invading Anglo-Normans (*c*1169 to 1225), the large stone fortresses of the period of territorial consolidation (*c*1175 to 1300), and the Late Medieval fortifications typified by the tower house. Later, fortified houses were erected, and while these are not true castles, they are included here for completeness since they predate the introduction of the large undefended house and are more akin to the stone castles that preceded them.

The earliest fortifications were of earth and timber and so could be constructed quickly. The most characteristic and common of these is the motte and bailey, while the ringwork also occurs but is less well known in Ireland.

MOTTES AND BAILEYS

A motte is a large flat-topped artificial earthen mound, usually sited on a natural height, with a wooden stockade around the perimeter of the summit, enclosing a wooden tower. The bailey or courtyard was a low earthen platform, usually rectangular in shape and situated to one side of the motte, but separated from it by a fosse or ditch which fully surrounded both structures. The bailey would also have been protected by a wooden palisade set into the inner rim of the

5

ditch. The ditches/fosses would frequently have been water-filled and access to the bailey would have been across a wooden bridge, usually a drawbridge. A second bridge would have been located to cross the ditch between the bailey and the motte and give access to steep steps leading to the gateway through the stockade on the summit of the mound.

Very few mottes and baileys in Ireland have been excavated and fewer still have been published, so our knowledge of them depends largely on historical references and field survey. Mottes were constructed very quickly provided a suitable natural mound could be found, and the speed of their erection coupled with the Normans' fighting skill meant that land quickly conquered could be securely held. The bailey was used for housing the soldiers, retainers and animals, while the lord or knight was probably housed on top of the motte. At Lismahon, Co Down, the remains of an almost square wooden house with a wooden watchtower attached to it were discovered on top of the mound. Excavations on top of the motte at Lurgenkeel, Co Louth, also produced traces of a wooden tower surrounded by a palisade. Another common feature found on the summits of mottes are pits around the periphery which were used as emplacements for archers. Ringforts, the defended homesteads of the Irish in the period *c* AD 500 to 1100, consisted of an enclosing fosse and bank and these were sometimes reused by the Anglo-Normans. At Dunsilly, Co Antrim, the enclosed area of the ringfort was levelled up and spoil from the surrounding ditch piled on the interior to raise a motte-like mound. Also at Lismahon and Rathmullan, Co Down, pre-existing ringforts were built up and fortified as mottes.

Mottes were sited at strategic points either along the borders of recently conquered land or guarding important routes. Clough Castle, Co Down, a motte and bailey that was erected around AD 1200, is situated close to the direct road from Downpatrick to Newry, a route that was probably followed by John de Courcy when he invaded Ulster in 1177. This route is also marked by the great motte and bailey known as the Crown Mound, near Newry, while Downpatrick has another strong motte castle, almost certainly built by de Courcy. In Drogheda, Hugh de Lacy built a large motte on Millmount about the time he established the town in 1186. Another de Lacy fortification dominates the area at Trim, Co Meath. However, the earliest Norman fortification there was probably a ringwork rather than a motte, despite a reference in the near-contemporary Norman-French poem *The Song of Dermot and the Earl* to the building of a fortified house, and a later reference during the reign of King John to the demolition of a tower on the site.

Mottes are more common in the eastern half of the country, and while they are concentrated in the areas controlled by the Anglo-Normans, they are strangely absent in some of the regions occupied by them, such as counties Cork and Limerick. Not every motte can be considered as the earliest Anglo-Norman fortress in a given area because in many instances they were also used at a secondary stage of colonisation, when the conquerors were consolidating their position. Few of the mottes of Ulster appear to have had a bailey, and where they did, it seems that they formed part of the main fortification for the soldiers, and not merely a protected area for servants and animals.

The owners of mottes in Ireland were not just from the upper social strata; some were of lower status and could come from quite far down the hierarchical scale. Nor would all of them have been of Anglo-Norman stock; there are at least sixteen mottes west of the Bann, an area controlled by the native Irish, whose owners clearly had begun to imitate the newcomers. In some instances Irish mounds of this type may have preceded the conquest. At Big Glebe in Co Derry, recent excavations produced evidence for this type of structure in the Early Medieval period, and in Co Monaghan there are a number of similar sites situated close to the Armagh border.

RINGWORKS

While the motte castles are easily recognisable, the ringwork castle is more difficult to identify. At its most basic it consisted of a raised area enclosed by a bank with a palisade around the top and an external ditch. Normally the only visible remains of a ringwork castle would be its earthen enclosing bank. It almost certainly had a strong timber gate-tower and a wooden tower in the interior; the ringwork castle depended on these for its main defences, whereas the motte's strength lay in its height. At Trim Castle the large central keep has a deep wide earth-cut fosse around it, except at the south where a gap through the defences was protected by a large stone tower. It would appear, therefore, that the keep at Trim was built on the ringwork castle that was erected by Hugh de Lacy in 1172. Excavations at Clonard, Co Meath, revealed the remains of a timber palisade associated with an embanked structure. The earthwork is undoubtedly the remains of a ringwork and is sited on the opposite bank of the River Deale to the Clonard motte.

Where mottes or ringworks were situated in newly established Anglo-Norman towns, they were often replaced subsequently by large stone-built fortresses such as those at Kilkenny, Trim, Athlone, Co Westmeath, Ferns, Co Wexford, and Adare, Co Limerick. This also happened to a lesser extent on rural sites, such as Clough Castle, Co Down, and Shanid, Co Limerick. However, in most instances after their initial use mottes were allowed to fall into disrepair, and they do not appear to have been occupied in Ireland much into the second quarter of the thirteenth century.

ANGLO-NORMAN STONE CASTLES

The principal Anglo-Norman stone-built fortresses, without the clutter of modern development that now surrounds most of them, must have been awe-inspiring sights. The great period of castle building in Ireland was from about AD 1190 to 1310, with the main phases of activity being around the turn of the twelfth and thirteenth centuries. The size and layout of castles of this period varied considerably depending on the suitability of the site and the availability of finance, skilled labour and materials such as stone. The siting of castles, therefore, sometimes represents a compromise between strategic requirements, access to building materials and resources to pay for the work.

8   The largest and best known fortresses of the early period are to be found in

the eastern half of Ireland, especially near the coast. Two of the greatest are Trim, Co Meath, and Carrickfergus, Co Antrim; the former built by Walter de Lacy, the latter by John de Courcy. Both reflect the power of those families in the early period of the conquest. These first stone castles were built to dominate and intimidate and, in the beginning, were seldom used as permanent residences. A detailed correlation of the historical and material evidence from Trim Castle, which has been partially excavated, gives a good insight into the building and fortification at this time.

TRIM CASTLE

Hugh de Lacy chose high ground at the west side of the River Boyne as the site for the fortification. According to the heroic poem of the conquest, *The Song of Dermot and the Earl*, he fortified a house at Trim in 1172 and threw a trench around it, and then enclosed it with a stockade. Excavation revealed that this early fortification was a type of ringwork rather than a motte. Hugh died in 1186 having built the first phase of the large stone keep or *donjon* and the curtain walls, and was succeeded by his son Walter, who by *c*1204 completed the massive stone castle that enclosed over three acres.

Three distinct phases of building can be seen in the keep and these have been closely dated from timbers recovered from the different levels of the structure. The first building phase was begun about AD 1175 when the massive central keep or *donjon*, the north-west gatehouse, the north angle tower and the other towers along the east curtain wall were built. The keep was built inside Hugh's ringwork, in the same way as the impressive one at Adare, Co Limerick. Stone for the structure was quarried from a massive moat cut into the bedrock immediately below the curtain wall, and dressed into rough ashlar blocks. It was heightened and large wooden galleries were attached to the outside of the walls in *c*1195 by Walter de Lacy, who finally topped it off to its present impressive height in *c*1204. The towers of the walls were clearly built in two phases, since those at the north and east sides of the site, including the gatehouse into the

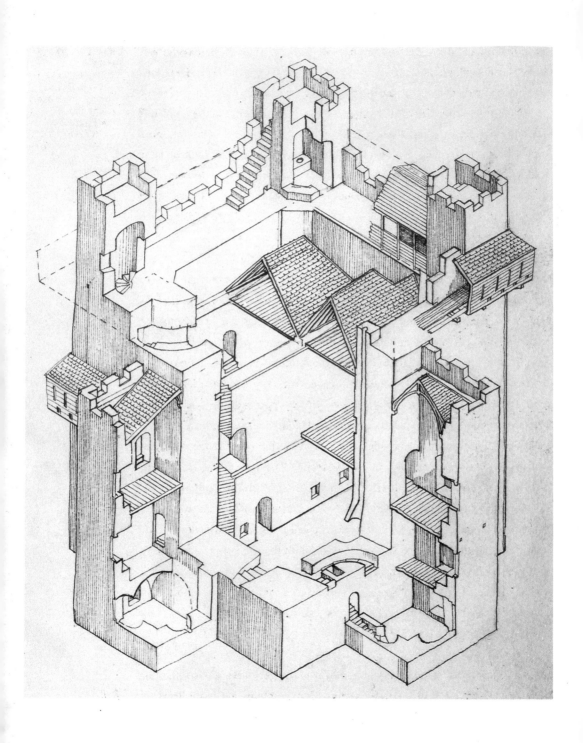

town of Trim and the great hall, are basically square in plan, whereas those at the west and south are D-shaped, the gatehouse here being circular and having a barbican (a fortified tower situated to the fore of the gateway).

It should be remembered that these large fortresses were roofed and had wooden galleries around their walls, which would make them far more impressive than the ruins one sees today. It also appears that many of these large castles were not used continuously as residences for the lord. The de Lacys, for instance, spent much of their time in Dublin or Drogheda. There was a practical reason for this: the castles, especially in the height of summer, would have been extremely smelly places considering that they lacked running water and flushing lavatories. Trim Castle was used as a residence when Geoffrey de Geneville, a French nobleman in the service of the king, married Matilda, granddaughter of Walter de Lacy, and made it his domain manor in 1254. De Lacy's granddaughter succeeded him at Trim because all his sons and grandsons had predeceased him — a clear indication of the poor survival rate of noble males in the medieval period (de Geneville's granddaughter also succeeded him). Archaeological excavations around the keep at Trim revealed that a large stone plinth had been added to it, probably by de Geneville to make it look grander. Ham Green pottery from Bristol and green-glazed wine jugs from France as well as iron arrowheads, silver coins and an iron axe (all dated to the thirteenth century) were found in the ditch around the keep.

Trim, like Adare, Co Limerick, King John's, Carlingford, Co Louth, Carrickfergus, Co Antrim, and Greencastle, Co Down, was built close to water for ease of access. At Adare, excavation revealed a mooring area close to the castle walls. In medieval times, because of difficult river crossings, it was very often faster to travel by boat where possible.

Photo 1 (Opposite) Trim Castle, Co Meath: cutaway reconstruction drawing of one of the later phases of building (c1200) showing the roof level inside the castle and the wooden hoarding.

KEEPS AND OTHER FEATURES

Large castles did not always have a keep. Living quarters were often within the towers of the curtain walls as well as in wooden structures inside the bawn or

11

enclosure. So-called keepless castles were for the most part constructed in the second half of the thirteenth century, and were often sited on high ground where bedrock was close to the surface. However, the keepless castles of the cities of Dublin, Limerick and Kilkenny were built in the first half of the thirteenth century. Dublin Castle had a royal writ issued for its erection in 1205, but building was still in progress in 1248, which gives a good indication of the length of time it took to complete these undertakings. It is also, incidentally, one of the few castles in Ireland that really was built on the instructions of King John.

Most of the keeps of the early period are almost square in plan, but at Greencastle, Co Down, and Carrickfergus, Co Antrim, there are large rectangular ones. Circular keeps occur at Dundrum, Co Down, Nenagh, Co Tipperary, and other sites, while at Athlone, Co Westmeath, and Castleknock, Co Dublin, there are polygonal examples. For defensive reasons the keep was normally entered through a door at first-floor level, and frequently there was a chapel on the second floor immediately above the entrance. The great hall, which was for the use of the lord and his family, was also situated at first-floor level, while their private chambers were on the floor above. Most of the servants and the soldiers would have occupied buildings within the ward or courtyard. At Trim Castle there is a separate hall with a vaulted area underneath for storing provisions, while at Adare there are two halls, and two kitchens in the outer ward, as well as other buildings.

Ferns Castle, Co Wexford, which was built by the Marshall family, is a large, impressive and prominently sited structure. It had a large rock-cut moat which provided the material for the building. When the immediate source of the material ran out, other stone was used, and this change in the masonry is obvious. Ferns is one of a small group of castles comprising substantial square or rectangular buildings with circular towers at the angles. Excavation at Ferns showed no evidence for internal stone structures, so they must have been made of wood. Traces of two drawbridges and outer defensive works were revealed, as well as evidence of a possible ringwork, which may have pre-dated the building of the castle. There is a very fine chapel in the second floor of the south-east angle tower. It is lighted by two trefoil-pointed windows and is covered by a vault with six moulded ribs springing from corbels which are in the form of capitals with truncated shafts. It was normal in these large castles to have a private chapel located at second-floor level, often directly over the first-floor entrance, as at Trim. Ferns produced good evidence for an outer bailey and defensive outworks of a type still to be seen at another of these castles at Lea, Co Laois.

Some of the most spectacular castles are situated on well-elevated rock sites, such as Roche, Co Louth, Dunamase, Co Laois, and Carlingford, Co Louth. Dunamase sits high up on a rock commanding a pass through the hills that divide the Laois plain and was previously a native Irish stronghold. Roche, built by the de Verdun family when they moved from Castletown near Dundalk, is sited on and encompasses a large rock outcrop that drops away dramatically on all but the east side. There, a ditch has been cut through the bedrock. The entrance to the castle is across this ditch and through an imposing gateway, flanked by half-round towers which are the remains of what was originally a massive gate-building. The interior of the castle has a large rectangular hall in the south-eastern angle. The tops of the walls have crenellations with arrow slits and square holes below them, which were used to carry a wooden hoard or gallery. These wooden galleries were a common feature and were constructed to project out from the walls so that the defenders could shoot arrows and drop stones on attackers below. King John's Castle, Carlingford, is also situated on rock outcrop which juts out into the lough, and must have offered considerable protection to the medieval town that lay just to its south.

Most of the later castles of the thirteenth century are keepless, their most impressive feature being a massive gate-building. This consisted of a pair of outwardly projecting half-round towers. Gate-buildings of this type were often added to earlier castles, and good examples can be seen at King John's, Limerick, Lea, Co Laois, and Castleroche, Co Louth. Roscommon town has probably the finest example of this type of castle, and Ballymote, Co Sligo, is also impressive. Roscommon Castle had a narrow moat around it, with a barbican and drawbridge protecting the south gate. At the north side there is a

13

cont. p 16

Photo 2 *A nineteenth-century drawing of Limerick Castle, Co Limerick, by W H Bartlett, showing the twin-towered gateway.*

14

Thefe trunckles heddes do playnly fhowe , eache rebeles fatall end,
And what a haynous crime it is , the Queene for to offend.

Although the theeues are plagued thus, by Princes trusty frendes,   6   For he that gouernes Irishe sople , presenting there her grace,
And brought for their innormyties, to sondry wretched endes: whose fame made rebelles often flye , the presence of his face:
Yet may not that a warning be, to those they leaue behinde,   He he I say, he goeth forth , with Marsis noble trayne,
But needes their treasons must appeare, long kept in festred mynde.   To instifie his Princes cause , but their demenures bayne:
Whereby the matter groweth at length, vnto a bloudy fielde,   Thus Queene he will haue honored, in middest of all her foes,
Euen to the rebells ouerthrow , except the traytours yelde.   And knowne to be a royall Prince, euen in despight of those.

Photo 3   *Sir Henry Sydney rides out of the gates of Dublin Castle, Co Dublin (no longer extant), the administrative centre for English rule and an early example of a keepless castle in Ireland.*

massive gateway with a D-shaped tower each side of the passageway, and with large towers at each angle. At Ballymote there were additional towers in the east and west walls, and excavation revealed the remains of the gate-building, which had been built with a double facing. This technique of double facing made it more difficult to breach the walls. Archaeological excavations at the south of Ballymote Castle demonstrated that there was no proper moat. Ballymote was built by de Burgh about 1300, but it soon fell into the hands of the Irish, who held it until 1584. About 16km (10 miles) north-west of Roscommon is Ballintober Castle, probably the largest of these late thirteenth-century keepless castles. Its plan is similar to Ballymote and Roscommon, but its gateway is small and it had polygonal towers at the angles of the curtain wall.

16

cont. p 32

Pl 1 *Knockgraffon Motte, Co Tipperary, an unusually tall and well-preserved earthwork castle.*

Pl 2 *Reconstruction drawing of a motte and bailey, the most common early Norman fortification.*

17

Pl 3   *Trim Castle, Co Meath, built by Walter de Lacy c1175, with its massive central keep and the south gate with barbican in the foreground. It later served as a meeting place for parliament and as a mint.*

18   Pl 4 (Opposite)   *Reconstruction drawing of the south gate and barbican of Trim Castle, Co Meath.*

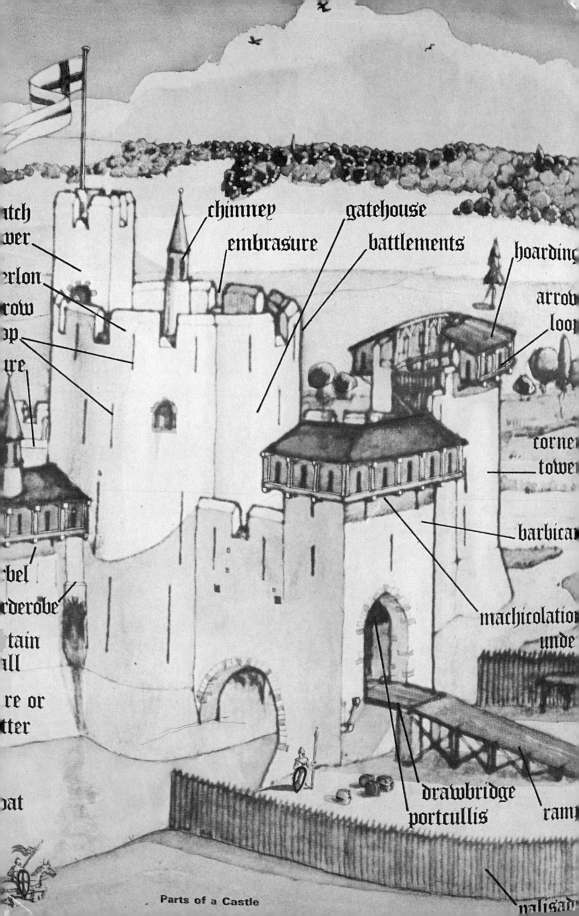

tch
wer

rlon

row

p

re

bel

rderobe

tain

ll

re or
tter

at

chimney

embrasure

gatehouse

battlements

hoarding

arrow
loop

corner
tower

barbica

machicolation
unde

drawbridge

portcullis

ram

Parts of a Castle

palisade

Pl 5   Roche Castle,
Co Louth, showing
the gateway and part
of the curtain wall,
with holes near the
top for carrying a
wooden hoard.

Pl 6   The gateway of
Roche Castle,
Co Louth, with its
massive D-shaped
towers.

20

Pl 7   *Dunamase Castle, Co Laois, a William Marshall fortress commanding the surrounding countryside.*

Pl 8   *Carrickfergus Castle, Co Antrim, the largest early Anglo-Norman fortress in the north of Ireland, probably built by John de Courcy.*

21

Pl 9 *Cloughoughter Castle, Co Cavan, an early circular castle sited on an island in Lough Oughter.*

22

23

Pl 10 Ballyloughan Castle, Co Carlow, a late thirteenth-century fortress with twin-towered gateway and rectangular hall at the left.

Pl 11 Ballymoon Castle, Co Carlow, an early fourteenth-century fortress, probably never completed.

24

Pl 12   *Roscommon Castle, Co Roscommon, the finest of the late thirteenth-century fortresses, with twin-towered gatehouses.*

Pl 13   *Cahir Castle, Co Tipperary, a large mainly fifteenth-century fortress sited at an important crossing of the River Suir.*

25

(Facing page)
Pl 15
*Ballagharahin
Castle, Co Laois,
tower house with
machicoulis over the
doorway and
bartisan on the angle
at the right. Both of
these defensive
structures allowed
arrows, stones and
the like to be dropped
on attackers below.*

Pl 16   *Athlumney Castle, Co Meath, a tower house with fortified residence attached at its left.*

Pl 17   *Doe Castle,
Co Donegal, a
sixteenth-century
castle with strong
bawn walls and
almost central tower.*

(Following pages)
Pl 18   *Donegal
Castle, Co Donegal,
a much-altered tower
house with a large
gable-fronted
seventeenth-century
house attached.*

29

cont. from p 16

Photo 4   *Nenagh Castle, Co Tipperary, with its circular keep and modern addition to the top.*

The later part of the thirteenth century and the beginning of the fourteenth century marks the end of the building of large Anglo-Norman fortresses. The lack of great castle building in the second half of the fourteenth and the first half of the fifteenth century, before the tower house appears on the landscape, can be accounted for by the Great European Famine (1315–17), the invasion of Ireland by Edward Bruce, and later by the bubonic plague, the Black Death (1348–50), which drastically reduced the population and hence the resources to build. Big castles were expensive — for instance, the total cost of building Roscommon Castle and refurbishing Rindown in Co Roscommon, and Athlone Castle, Co Westmeath, was just over £3,000. The English kings who provided most of the finance had other preoccupations at home in the fourteenth century, and they were constantly short of cash.

32

cont. p 36

Photo 5   *Ferns Castle, Co Wexford, after conservation. Note the excavated portion of the moat in front of the castle.*

Photo 6
Thirteenth-century stone head found in the moat of Ferns Castle, Co Wexford.

33

(Facing page)
Photo 7   *The chapel of Ferns Castle, Co Wexford, with its fine groined roof.*

Photo 8
Reconstruction drawing of a wooden hoard on a curtain wall. Wooden hoards or galleries enabled defenders to shoot arrows and drop stones on attackers below.

35

(Facing page)
Photo 9 *Typical tower house two-centred arch over doorway leading to spiral staircase.*

By the beginning of the fifteenth century, when castle building resumed on a large scale, the predominant form was the tower house, more a strong private residence than a military fortification. There are, however, a number of large castles that reflect the building traditions of the early stone fortresses, such as Cahir, Co Tipperary. This is the largest of these Late Medieval castles and has within its high curtain walls three courtyards, a hall and a massive keep. In some instances, such as Askeaton, Co Limerick, an early castle was refortified and expanded in the fifteenth century.

TOWER HOUSES

The tower house is a common feature of the Irish landscape and could be described as the typical residence of the Irish gentry in the fifteenth and sixteenth centuries. The fact that it is generally seen as a fortified house rather than a true castle is an over-simplification based on examples in the eastern half of the country; in western counties such as Galway, Clare and Limerick, and Cork in the south, there are very large and complex structures that are more akin to proper castles than mere fortified residences.

The tower house at its most simple consisted of a stone tower, normally rectangular in plan, up to six storeys high, with various defensive elements, including a defended courtyard. In 1429 Henry VI introduced a £10 grant to subsidise the building of tower houses in the 'Pale' (an area comprising parts of Dublin, Kildare, Louth and Meath) and this seems to be the reason why there were so many basic types built in the east of the country, especially within the Pale. Typical of the smaller type tower house are those found in Co Louth, such as Killincoole, Milltown and Roodstown. They are all four storeys high, rectangular in shape, with towers projecting from two opposing angles, one to carry the stairs, the other the garderobe (privy) and with a stone-built barrel-shaped vault over the ground floor. The accommodation in these simple tower houses consisted of a hall directly over the barrel-vaulted ground floor and private chambers on the levels above. Access to all chambers would have been

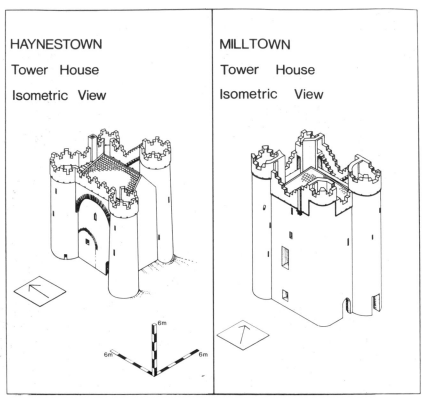

HAYNESTOWN

Tower   House

Isometric   View

MILLTOWN

Tower   House

Isometric   View

6m

6m   6m

Photo 10   *Isometric drawings of two typical Co Louth tower houses. The exterior of Haynestown clearly shows the arch of the barrel vault over the ground floor. The roof position in relation to the wall-walk and battlement should be noted.*

from the spiral stairs in one of the projecting towers. The main doorway, which is always at ground-floor level, gave access to both the stairwell and the ground floor. The entranceways at the ground-floor level were protected by murder-holes (rectangular openings in the stone ceilings through which arrows could be shot or debris dumped to repel invaders). The strong wooden doors could also be barred from the inside and an iron grill (a yett) pulled across the front of the door with chains. On the outside of the wall above the doorway, usually at battlement level, was placed a small stone chamber called a machicoulis, which projected out from the wall face and was carried on corbels. From inside this, arrows could be fired down between the corbels, or stones dropped on anyone

38

Photo 11   *Two windows from the Mint, Carlingford, Co Louth, a small late sixteenth-century tower house.*

attempting to break down the door. Similar features for protecting the corners are called bartisans. Another feature of tower houses is their base-batter, which is the outward splay of the bottom portion of the wall whereby stones dropped from the battlements would rebound and hit the attackers. The windows at ground floor level consisted of splayed slit openings to allow arrows to be fired outwards, while some of the later sixteenth-century examples had loops for guns.

Accommodation was fairly primitive — there was no running water and the garderobes were merely wooden seats over stone chutes in the walls, which exited outside the wall close to the ground. The garderobes were in small

39

cont. p 42

Photo 12   *Aughnanure Castle, tower house, Co Galway, a sixteenth-century stronghold on the shores of Lough Corrib, with much of its bawn wall and towers remaining.*

Photo 13   *Corbel with woman's face used for supporting a wooden beam in Carntown tower house, Co Louth.*

40

Photo 14   *Ballagharahin Castle, Co Laois, showing bartisan protecting the corner. Note the different types of heads on the two-light windows.*

41

cont. from p 39

chambers and sometimes contained a slop-stone, for hand washing, the water from which also drained through the wall. In the more elaborate tower houses such as Bunratty, Co Clare, and Blarney, Co Cork, the layout is much more complex and there are numerous passages within the walls, small chambers, several stairwells and many vaulted floor levels.

The upper levels of most tower houses comprised the living and sleeping quarters of the owner, and these had much larger and more decorative windows, unlike the simple defensive slits of the ground floor. They also contained large stone fireplaces, usually set in the gable ends of the building, with their flues taken through the walls and carried upwards on the outside on corbels above the level of the parapets. Many tower houses are still lived in today and have modern houses attached to them. In some instances the tower house has been abandoned or used as a farm building while a new house has been erected close by.

It should not be forgotten that probably all of these dwellings would have had a defended courtyard surrounded by a stone wall, with small towers at the angles. Within the courtyards or bawns there would have been wooden buildings, some free-standing and others built against the curtain walls.

FORTIFIED HOUSES

Towards the end of the sixteenth century and in the early seventeenth century, a new type of castle evolved, the semi-fortified house. Features of these houses, which were usually symmetrical, include gables with massive lozenge/diamond-shaped chimney stacks and mullioned and transomed windows. The presence of defensive galleries and loops, as well as a surrounding bawn wall, are indicative of their design to repel an attack. One of the earliest and most important of these is Rathfarnham Castle, Co Dublin, which was built in *c*1589. But perhaps the most perfect and also the latest example is that at Burntcourt, Co Tipperary, which was built in 1650. It has twenty-six gables, numerous tall chimney stacks, large mullioned and transomed windows with hood-mouldings, and clear

Photo 15 *Burntcourt, Co Tipperary, a fortified house.*

Photo 16 *Fireplace at Donegal Castle, Co Donegal. The carving includes the arms of Sir Basil Brooke and the strapwork and festoons popular in the ornament of the period.*

43

Photo 17 *Portumna Castle, Co Galway, a fortified house dating from the early seventeenth century and built by the fourth Earl of Clanricarde, now partially restored after a fire destroyed its interior in 1826.*

evidence of stone corbels designed to carry a wooden gallery around the outside of the walls. The builders of these structures were concerned with providing a house of formal and symmetrical plan on Renaissance lines which answered a desire for more luxurious living standards but sacrificed nothing of the defensive nature of the structure. They were designed to give flanking cover from towers on the angles and many had machicolations and bartisans as well as well-defended bawns. A logical development from the tower houses and retaining many of their defensive features, they marked the end of true castle building in Ireland.

By the middle of the seventeenth century strong houses which also retain some defensive features of the tower house come into vogue, but they lack bawn walls, crenellations, mural stairs and passages, which are common features of the earlier structures. However, it was probably the advent of gunpowder and siege guns as much as changing fashions that rang the death knell of the true castle.

44

Bailey: A courtyard which is attached to a castle. In the case of an earthwork castle, it is situated to one side and is defended by earthen banks with wooden palisades and an external fosse (ditch), which in the case of a motte separates the castle mound from the bailey. Stone castles have their baileys defended by stone walls with towers and an external moat.

Barbican: A fortified tower defending the gate of a castle or city.

Bartisan: Similar to the MACHICOLATION but located on the corners of tower houses.

Base-batter: The outward splay of the bottom portion of the wall of a stone tower whereby stones dropped from the battlements would rebound and hit the attackers.

Bawn: The walled courtyard of a tower house, sometimes provided with corner towers for improved defence.

Cashel: A circular drystone enclosure common in Early Medieval Ireland, especially in rocky districts.

Corbel: A stone block projecting from a wall, used to support a wooden beam.

Curtain wall: The outer defensive wall of a castle.

Earthwork: A structure made mainly of heaped earth, usually banks, ditches and mounds. Often used to denote defensive works.

Fosse: A ditch.

Garderobe: A privy consisting of a wooden seat over a stone chute in the wall of a round tower, which exited outside the wall close to the ground.

Hoard/Hoarding: A feature of Anglo-Norman castles, constructed to project out from the walls so that the defenders could shoot arrows and drop stones on attackers below.

Keep: The principal tower of a castle, normally free-standing, with living quarters. Also known as a *donjon*.

Machicolation/ Machicoulis: A small stone chamber supported on corbels situated on the outside wall of a tower house, normally above the doorway, from which stones etc could be dropped on attackers.

Mullion:	A vertical post or stone dividing a window into two or more 'lights' (openings).
Palisade:	Fence of stakes.
Retainer:	Follower/dependant of a lord.
Ringfort:	A round, ditched site, built to protect the homesteads of the Irish in the period *c* AD 500 to 1100.
Transom:	A horizontal bar of wood or stone across a window or panel.
Ward:	The courtyard of a castle.

SELECT BIBLIOGRAPHY

Platt, C. *The Castle in Medieval England and Wales*. London, 1982.

Renn, D. *Norman Castles in Britain*. John Baker, London, 1973.

Kenyon, J R. *Medieval Fortifications*. Leicester University Press, London, 1990.

Higham, R & Barker, P. *Timber Castles*. Batsford, London, 1992.

Johnson, D N. *The Irish Castle*. Eason & Sons, Dublin, 1985.
   Irish Castles. Folens, Dublin.

Leask, H G. *Irish Castles*. Dundalgan Press Ltd, Dunkalk, 1977.

Ryan, M (ed). *Irish Archaeology Illustrated*. Country House, Dublin, 1994.

46

INDEX